Contents

Reading	Caterpillar's Voice	4
Activities		5
Initial Sounds		6
Capital Letters		7
Reading	Brown Hares	8
Activities		9
Initial Sounds		10
Using Words		11
Reading	The Foolish Crow	12
Activities		13
Vowel Sounds		14
Full Stops		15
Reading	The Silver on the Hearth	16
Activities		17
Vowel Sounds		18
Capital Letters		19
Reading	All for a Pansa	20
Activities		21
Revision		22
Capital Letters		23
Reading	Robert the Bruce and the Spider	24
Activities		25
Initial Blends		26
Capital Letters		27
Reading	The Boy who Cried Wolf	28
Activities		29
Phonics		30
Grammar		31
Reading	The Turnip	32
Activities		33
Word Families		34
Grammar		35
Reading	The Lion and the Mouse	36
Activities		37
Phonics		38
Questions		39
Reading	Fire Wrapped in Paper	40
Activities		41
Word Endings: 'ck'		42
Grammar		43
Reading	Tigers	44
Activities		45
Word Endings: 'ing'		46
Grammar		47
Reading	The Real Princess	48
Activities		49
Phonics		50
Questions		51
Reading	Chimpanzees	52
Activities		53
Word Endings: 'ss', 'll'		54
Capital Letters		55
Reading	Sheep	56
Activities		57
Phonics		58
Compound Words		59
Reading	The Hedgehog	60
Activities		61
Final Blends		62
Compound Words		63
Reading	The Crow and the Jug	64
Activities		65
Final Blends		66
Grammar		67
Reading	The Fox and the Goat	68
Activities		69
Word Endings: 'all'		70
Using Words		71
Reading	The Circus Comes To Town	72
Activities		73
Word Endings: 'y'		74
Grammar		75
Reading	Taking a Donkey to Market	76
Activities		77
Phonics		78
Grammar		79
Puzzle Page		80

Reading

 Read the story. Colour the picture.

Caterpillar's Voice
(a traditional story of the Maasai people from East Africa)

One day, Caterpillar hid in Hare's house.
When Hare came home, he called, "Who's there?"
"I'm an elephant eater!" said Caterpillar in a big voice.
Hare was scared. He asked his friends Jackal, Rhino and Elephant to help, but they were all too frightened.
Then a little frog came along. "I'll help you, Hare," he said. "Who's there?" he shouted.
Caterpillar yelled, "I'm an elephant eater!"
Frog shouted, in an even bigger voice, "Good! I eat elephant eaters!"
"Oh, help!" said Caterpillar and ran away. Hare and Frog saw him and laughed. Why had everyone been so scared of such a tiny animal?

English Skills 1

Published by Collins
An imprint of HarperCollins*Publishers*
The News Building
1 London Bridge Street
London
SE1 9GF

Browse the complete Collins catalogue at
www.collins.co.uk

© HarperCollins*Publishers* Limited 2011, on behalf of the author
First published in 2006 by Folens Limited.

ISBN-13: 978-0-00-743718-4

Any educational institution that has purchased one copy of this publication may make unlimited duplicate copies for use exclusively within that institution. Permission does not extend to reproduction, storage within a retrieval system, or transmittal in any form or by any means, electronic, mechanical, photocopying, recording or otherwise, of duplicate copies for loaning, renting or selling to any other institution without the permission of the Publisher.

British Library Cataloguing in Publication Data
A catalogue record for this publication is available from the British Library.

Every effort has been made to trace copyright holders and to obtain their permission for the use of copyright material. The authors and publishers will gladly receive any information enabling them to rectify any error or omission in subsequent editions.

Editor: Geraldine Sowerby
Layout artist: Patricia Hollingsworth
Illustrations: Tony Randall
Cover design: Martin Cross
Editorial consultant: Helen Whittaker

Printed and bound by CPI Group (UK) Ltd, Croydon, CR0 4YY

Activities

A Write **yes** or **no**.

1. Hare hid in Caterpillar's house. _____

2. Caterpillar had a big voice. _____

3. Frog was too scared to help. _____

4. Caterpillar said he was an elephant eater. _____

5. Caterpillar ran away. _____

B Write the correct word.

voice   elephant   house   animal   eater

1. Caterpillar was a tiny _____ .

2. Caterpillar said he was an elephant _____ .

3. Frog had an even bigger _____ than Caterpillar.

4. Caterpillar hid in Hare's _____ .

5. The _____ was too scared to help.

C Write the missing word.

h _ _ _ _   a _ _ _ _ _

v _ _ _ _   e _ _ _ _ _ _ _

Initial Sounds

A Write the initial sounds.

Capital Letters

 A Write the lower case letters for these capital letters.

T	B	M	D	Z	G	S	H	R	Q	F	I	X	L	P

> We use capital letters at the start of a sentence.

 B Ring the capital letter at the start of each sentence.

1. Ann was reading a book.
2. My daddy ate an egg.
3. An elephant is a very big animal.
4. I fell off my chair.
5. An apple a day keeps the doctor away.
6. I need an umbrella for the rain.
7. My mum is a teacher.

C Write these sentences correctly.

1. here comes the bus.   Here_____
2. it is a very sunny day.   _____
3. we love ice cream.   _____
4. the children are playing. _____
5. your bag is in the hall.   _____

Reading

 Read about brown hares. Colour the picture.

Brown Hares

Brown hares look a lot like rabbits. They have long ears with black tips. In winter their fur is dark brown but in summer it is a lighter colour.

Brown hares are larger than rabbits and have longer legs. They can run very fast. They like to live in flat, grassy places.

Brown hares eat wild flowers in summer and grass in winter. They also like to eat farmers' crops.

A hare's home is called a form. It is a dip in the ground where the hare hides from animals that hunt it. Baby hares are born in the spring and are called leverets. There are about four leverets in a litter.

Activities

A Write **yes** or **no**.

1. Brown hares look a lot like rabbits. _____
2. Brown hares have black fur. _____
3. Brown hares have short ears. _____
4. A brown hare's home is called a form. _____
5. Brown hares like to live in trees. _____
6. Brown hares eat mice. _____
7. Baby hares are called leverets. _____
8. Brown hares eat grass in winter. _____

B Try this wordsearch.

hare   winter
ears   form
colour   grass
crops   summer
flowers   spring

h	e	l	b	o	k	g	c
a	a	n	h	m	c	r	o
l	r	r	a	m	f	a	l
o	s	f	e	g	o	s	o
w	i	n	t	e	r	s	u
e	e	s	u	m	m	e	r
r	s	p	r	i	n	g	d
s	c	s	c	r	o	p	s

© HarperCollins Publishers Limited 2011   English Skills 1

Initial Sounds

A Ring the correct initial sound.

B Write the missing letter.

Using Words

 A Unscramble these sentences.

1. going Ann to school is.

   _____

2. Jim run can fast.

   _____

3. teacher nice very is My.

   _____

4. live a house I in.

   _____

5. sunny It a day is.

   _____

6. read I can story a.

   _____

 B Write **of** or **off**.

Examples: I had two cups **of** tea.
I fell **off** my bicycle.

1. I am afraid _____ the dark.

2. I need a lot _____ money.

3. Get _____ that wall!

4. Six _____ the children are sick.

5. I would like six _____ those apples.

6. I was pushed _____ the chair.

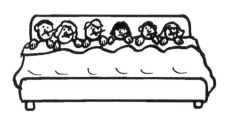

Reading

A Read the story. Colour the pictures.

The Foolish Crow

1

One day a crow sat on the roof of a house.

2

She saw some cheese. The cheese was on a bird-table.

3

The crow took the cheese. She went to a tree. She was going to eat the cheese.

4

A hungry fox saw the crow. He wanted the cheese. He had a good idea.

5

"Hello, Mrs Crow," he said. "You look pretty!" The crow was very pleased. She nodded her head.

6

"Oh, Mrs Crow," said the fox, "you must be a lovely singer!" The crow was very very pleased. She began to sing. The cheese fell. The fox ran off with it and ate it!

Activities

A Write **yes** or **no**.

1. The crow saw some cheese. _____
2. The cheese was on the ground. _____
3. The crow sat on a roof. _____
4. A rabbit saw the crow. _____
5. The fox told the crow that she was pretty. _____
6. The fox ate the crow. _____

B Write the missing word. Colour the pictures.

C Choose the correct word.

1. The crow saw some _____. (bread, cheese, milk)
2. A _____ (dog, wolf, fox) saw the crow.
3. The fox told the crow that she was _____. (ugly, bad, pretty)
4. The fox _____ (ate, cooked, left) the cheese.
5. The crow was a _____ (clever, wise, silly) bird.
6. The fox was a _____ (stupid, clever, silly) animal.

Vowel Sounds

A Write **a** or **i**.

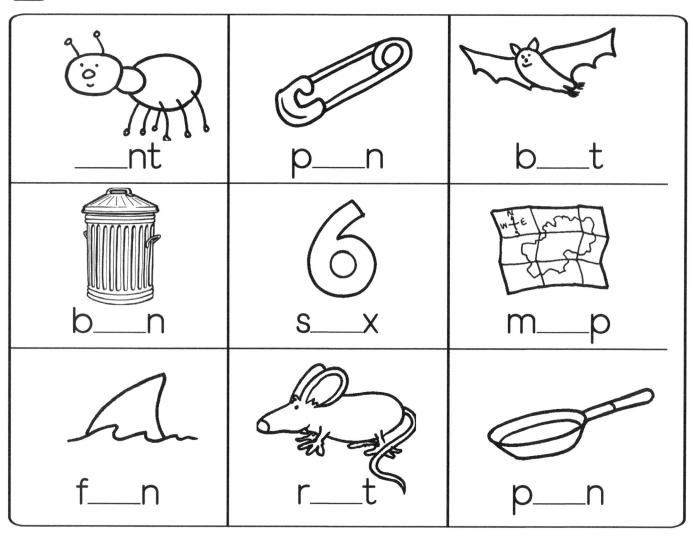

___nt	p___n	b___t
b___n	s___x	m___p
f___n	r___t	p___n

B Write the correct word.

tip tap	jim jam	mit mat
———	———	———
tin tan	min man	fin fan
———	———	———

Full Stops

We put a full stop at the end of a sentence.

 A Put a full stop at the end of each sentence.

1. I want to look at the television

2. He asked me about the book

3. I fell off my bike

4. My mum gave it to me

5. I am waiting for the bus

6. She pushed me into the water

 B Write the sentences. Put in the capital letters and full stops.

1. the boy ran across the road

2. my name is Tom

3. his mum is in hospital

4. the house was burnt down

5. we will meet at the shop

6. he eats too many sweets

Reading

A Read the story. Colour the picture.

The Silver on the Hearth
(a traditional story from Afghanistan)

Once there was a poor farmer who wished for silver on his hearth. One day he found a big pot full of silver coins in a field. He thought, "I wished for silver on my hearth. This money must belong to somebody else."

When the farmer told his wife about the pot of coins, she was angry. She talked to the man next door. "If you get the pot for me I will share the coins with you," she said.

The neighbour found the pot, but when he looked inside it was full of snakes! He thought the farmer's wife had tricked him. That night he threw the snakes down the farmer's chimney. When the farmer got up in the morning he found a big pile of silver coins on his hearth. His wish had come true.

Activities

A Write **yes** or **no**.

1. The farmer was rich. _____
2. He wished for silver on his hearth. _____
3. He found a big pot full of gold coins. _____
4. His wife was angry. _____
5. The neighbour found snakes in the pot. _____
6. He threw the snakes down the farmer's chimney. _____
7. The snakes turned into silver coins. _____

B Write the correct word.

farmer   silver   field
chimney   tricked   wish

1. The _____ was poor.
2. The farmer found the pot in a _____ .
3. The neighbour thought the wife had _____ him.
4. The farmer's _____ came true.
5. The pot was full of _____ coins.
6. The neighbour threw the snakes down the _____ .

C Write the missing word.

n _ _ _ _ _ _ _ _   w _ _ _

c _ _ _ _   p _ _

Vowel Sounds

A Write **e**, **o** or **u**.

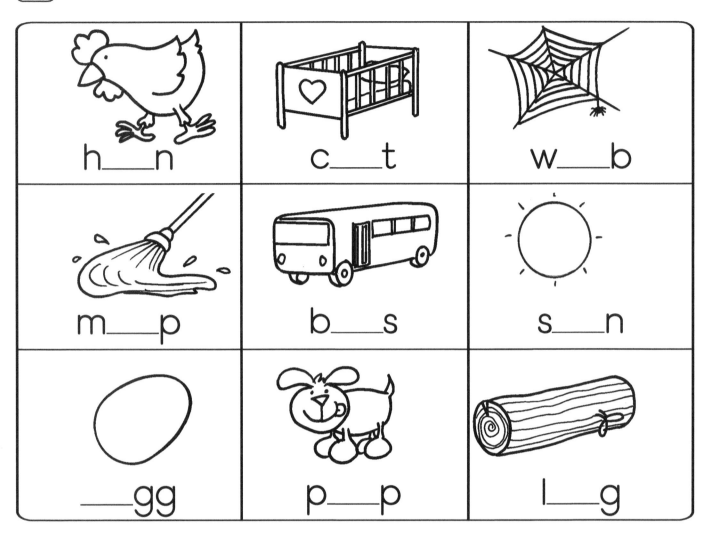

B Write the correct word.

nut net not	pet pot put	reg rog rug
net		

bex box bux	ten ton tun	net not nut

Capital Letters

> We use capital letters for names.
> Example: **M**eg and **T**om are twins.

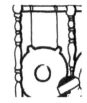

A Write these sentences correctly.

1. today is ben's birthday.

   _____

2. tom and emma like running.

   _____

3. halah and bahir went to school.

   _____

4. jim and pat are in the park.

   _____

5. lin is playing with kim.

   _____

6. i have a fish called spot.

   _____

B Unscramble the letters and write the names.

inL Lin	eBn ____	miJ ____
imK ____	hiraB ____	omT ____

Reading

A Read the story. Colour the picture.

All for a Pansa
(a traditional story from India)

Once there was a rich man who wanted to find out how clever his son Sanjay was. He gave Sanjay a pansa, a tiny coin, and told him to buy just one thing. The thing had to be something to eat, something to drink, something to chew on, something to plant in the garden, and food for the cow.

On the way to market, Sanjay met a girl. She asked him why he looked so worried and he told her. "That's easy," said the girl. "Buy a watermelon. That is something to eat, something to drink, something to chew on, something to plant in the garden, and food for the cow."

So Sanjay bought a watermelon. His father was pleased. "You are very clever," he said. "I'm not clever," said Sanjay. "A girl told me what to do."

Sanjay's father asked the girl and her family to come to dinner. Sanjay married the girl and they lived happily ever after.

Activities

A Write **yes** or **no**.

1. The man was poor. _____
2. He asked Sanjay to buy just one thing. _____
3. The thing had to be something to drink. _____
4. The thing had to be something to sit on. _____
5. Sanjay bought a cow. _____
6. Sanjay's father was pleased. _____

B Write the missing words. Colour the pictures.

The rich man gave his _____ a _____ .

Sanjay met a _____ on the way to _____ .

Sanjay _____ a _____ .

Sanjay and the girl got _____ .

Revision

A Write the initial letter.

B Write **a**, **e**, **i**, **o** or **u**.

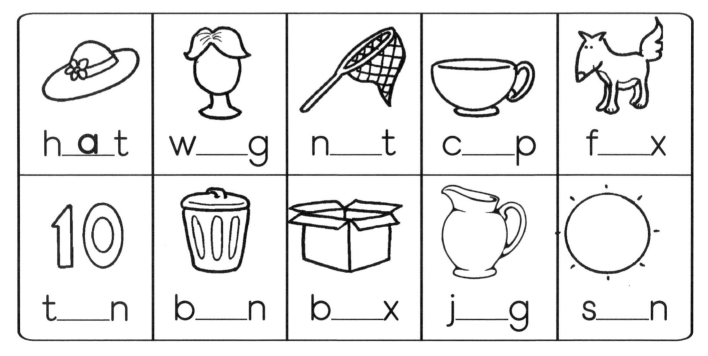

Capital Letters

We use capital letters for names of places.
Examples: **A**frica, **C**hina, **M**oscow, **N**ew **Y**ork.

 A Write these sentences correctly.

1. Latif lives in cairo.

2. I live in england.

3. Kim went to paris.

4. It is cold in iceland.

5. Ben loves going to hong kong.

B Find the place names in the wordsearch.

Tokyo   Iceland
New York   Cuba
Cairo   Asia
England   Africa

y	E	n	g	l	a	n	d
l	N	k	o	N	T	o	o
c	A	e	l	n	o	k	C
e	f	E	w	d	k	C	u
l	r	l	a	Y	y	a	b
a	i	Y	r	v	o	i	a
n	c	n	a	T	i	r	c
d	a	A	s	i	a	o	k

© HarperCollins Publishers Limited 2011   English Skills 1

Reading

A Read the story. Colour the picture.

Robert the Bruce and the Spider

(a traditional story from Scotland)

Once there was a King of Scotland called Robert the Bruce. The King of England sent a big army to Scotland. Robert the Bruce fought the English six times but his army lost every time.

One day when he was hiding in a cave, Robert the Bruce saw a spider trying to spin her web. The spider tried six times to make her thread stick to the wall of the cave. It would not stick. On the seventh time, the thread stuck to the wall. The spider could spin her web.

The spider gave Robert the Bruce hope. "I will try a seventh time too," he said. He fought the English a seventh time. This time he won and the King of England went back home.

Activities

A Write **yes** or **no**.

1. Robert the Bruce was the King of England. _____
2. Robert the Bruce lost six times. _____
3. Robert the Bruce hid in a shed. _____
4. He saw a spider trying to spin her web. _____
5. The spider gave up. _____
6. Robert the Bruce won the seventh time. _____

B Choose the correct word.

1. The King of England sent an _____ (ant, army, elephant) to Scotland.
2. Robert the Bruce _____ (looked, liked, lost) six times.
3. He saw a _____ (spider, web, bat) in a cave.
4. The spider did not _____ (sit, give, stand) up.
5. The spider gave Robert the Bruce _____ . (money, presents, hope)
6. The King of England _____ (went, saw, was) back home.

C Write the missing word.

S _ _ _ _ _ _ _ _   C _ _ _

S _ _ _ _ _   E _ _ _ _ _ _

Initial Blends

A Ring the correct initial sounds.

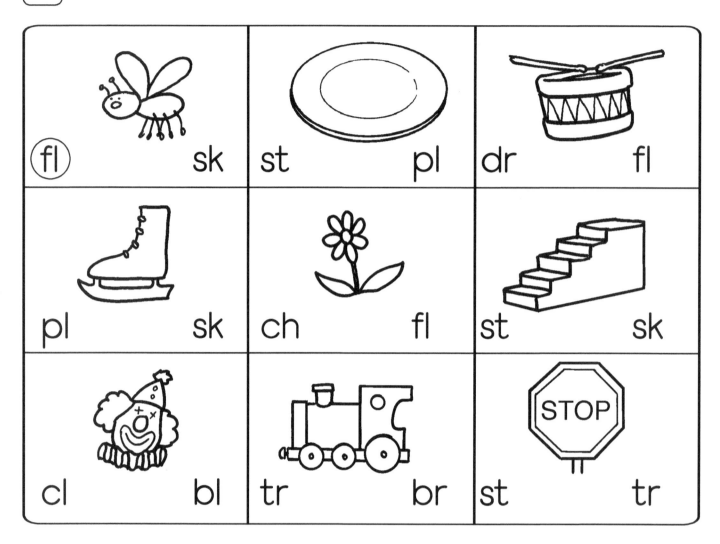

Capital Letters

> We use capital letters for days and months.
> Examples: **M**onday, **W**ednesday, **M**ay, **J**une.

 Underline the words which need a capital letter.

1. Peter got a new coat on tuesday.
2. I will have a present for you on friday.
3. may is my favourite month.
4. My birthday is in march.
5. Dad's birthday is in july.
6. Ann got a big balloon on monday.

 Write these sentences correctly.

1. On monday we start school.

2. january is the first month of the year.

3. Sunil's birthday is in august.

4. It is my birthday on sunday.

5. I am going on holiday in may.

6. Mum went to the doctor on tuesday.

Reading

 Read the story. Colour the picture.

The Boy who Cried Wolf

Once there was a boy who looked after sheep on a hill.
One day, he said to himself, "I am so bored! Just for fun I will call Wolf! Wolf! People will come running."

So he called Wolf! Wolf! Many people came running. "Ha, ha, ha," he laughed, "it was only a joke." He did this three times. Each time the people came he told them that it was only a joke. There was no wolf.

But, one day, the wolf did come. "Help! help! The wolf is here," the boy cried. But the people said, "We know that there is no wolf. That boy is only playing a joke. There is no danger. This time we will not go!"
So the people did not go and the wolf killed all the sheep.

Activities

A Write **yes** or **no**.

1. The boy was looking after sheep. _____

2. The boy loved his job. _____

3. One day the boy called, "Goat! Goat!" _____

4. The people came running. _____

5. He called "wolf" six times. _____

6. The boy killed the wolf. _____

B Choose the correct word for each sentence.

1. The boy was looking after _____. (sheep, geese, goats)

2. The boy was on a _____. (farm, hill, lorry)

3. The boy was _____. (happy, sad, bored)

4. The boy cried _____ (help!, wolf!, danger!)

5. The people did not _____. (eat, go, drink)

6. The wolf killed _____. (the boy, the sheep, the people)

Phonics

A Ring the correct initial sounds.

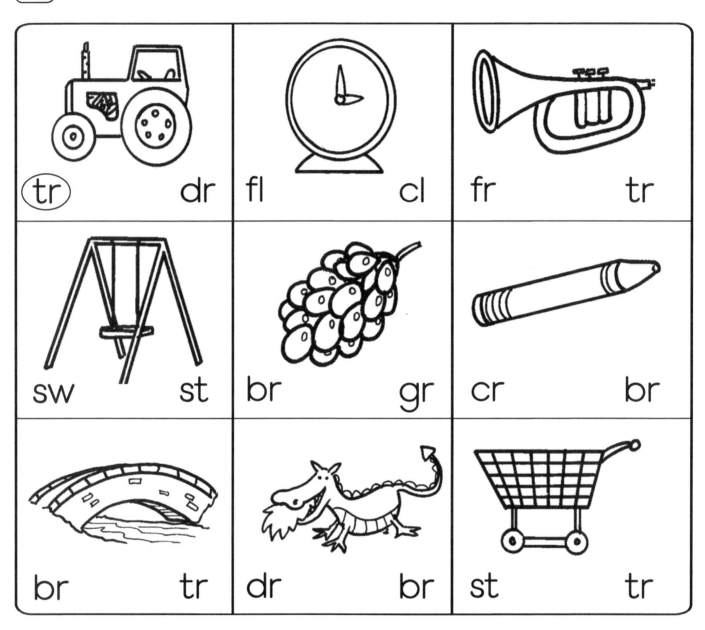

B Write the correct missing letters for each word.

dr   fr   cr

___ og   ___ um   ___ ab

Grammar

> We use a capital letter for the word 'I'.
> Example: **I** like this book.

 Ring the capital letter **I** in each sentence.

1. Ann and I are going home.
2. I am getting a new coat.
3. Abid and I have the same birthday.
4. I have a cousin called Pat.
5. My sister and I have long hair.
6. I can hear the music playing.

B Write these sentences correctly.

1. Tom and i are going fishing.

___

2. i like drawing pictures.

___

3. i will buy you a pencil.

___

4. You and i can run.

___

5. Mina and i lost the race.

___

6. i am going on holiday.

___

Reading

A Read the story. Colour the picture.

The Turnip

(a traditional story from Russia)

An old man planted a turnip. The turnip grew very big. The old man tried to pull it up, but it didn't move. He got his wife.

The old woman grabbed the old man and the old man grabbed the turnip. They pulled and pulled, but the turnip didn't move. So the old woman got the dog. The dog grabbed the old woman, the old woman grabbed the old man and the old man grabbed the turnip. They pulled and pulled, but the turnip didn't move. So the dog got the cat.

The cat grabbed the dog, the dog grabbed the old woman, the old woman grabbed the old man and the old man grabbed the turnip. They pulled and pulled and… crash! They all fell over. They had pulled up the turnip!

Activities

A Write **yes** or **no**.

1. The old man planted a turnip. _____
2. The turnip didn't grow very big. _____
3. The old woman got the dog. _____
4. The dog grabbed the cat. _____
5. They all fell over. _____
6. They pulled up the turnip. _____

B Write the correct word in each box.

dog   turnip   old man   cat

Word Families

A Make word families.

hat	fun	hop
__at (mat)	__un (sun)	__op (mop)
__at (bat)	__un (bun)	__op (pop)
__at (cat)	__un (run)	__op (top)

hug	den	but
__ug (jug)	__en (ten)	__ut (hut)
__ug (rug)	__en (hen)	__ut (nut)
__ug (mug)	__en (pen)	__ut (cut)

gap	win	pan
__ap (map)	__in (pin)	__an (can)
__ap (cap)	__in (fin)	__an (man)
__ap (tap)	__in (bin)	__an (van)

Grammar

We use a question mark if the sentence asks a question.
Examples: Where? What? Who? Why? When? How?

A Trace over these question marks.

B Write a question mark at the end of each sentence.

1. Where are you
2. Who is there
3. Why are you angry
4. Is Tom at home
5. How are you
6. What time is it

C Write a question mark or a full stop at the end of each sentence.

1. Where is my coat
2. The cat is asleep
3. Is it a good book
4. What is it
5. The baby is happy
6. The frog is jumping

Reading

 A Read the story. Colour the picture.

The Lion and the Mouse

One day a lion was asleep under a tree. A little mouse ran over his paw. The lion lifted his paw to kill the mouse. "Please, please, do not kill me," squeaked the mouse.

The lion took pity on her.

"Thank you," said the mouse. "One day I will help you."

"Ha, ha, ha," laughed the lion. "A little mouse like you, could not help the King of the Jungle!" A few days later, the lion walked into a trap. He roared and roared. Suddenly, he heard a little squeak. It was the mouse. She nibbled at the ropes. Soon the lion was free.
The lion thanked the mouse.

"You have saved my life," he said. The lion and the mouse became great friends.

Activities

A Write **yes** or **no**.

1. The lion was asleep under a bed. _____
2. A rat ran over the lion's paw. _____
3. The lion took pity on the mouse. _____
4. The lion walked into a shop. _____
5. The mouse nibbled at the cheese. _____
6. The lion thanked the mouse. _____

B Write the correct word.

C Choose the correct word.

1. A lion is a wild _____. (dog, rat, cat)
2. The lion is the king of _____. (the castle, the country, the jungle)
3. The lion walked into a _____. (house, farm, trap)
4. The mouse _____ (nibbled, tore, broke) the rope.
5. The lion _____ (thanked, killed, ate) the mouse.

Phonics

A Write the correct initial sounds **gr pl dr br bl**.

B Choose the correct word for each sentence.

1. I saw a _____ (dragon, drum) in his cave.

2. I was hungry and ate some _____. (grass, grapes)

3. I swept the floor with the _____. (brick, brush)

4. Amira wore a green _____. (dragon, dress)

5. I gave the _____. (plug, plant) some water

6. Coal is _____. (blood, black)

Questions

 A Write a question mark.

1. Where is my homework
2. Who is going to your party
3. When are you going on holiday
4. Why are you digging over there

B Write the correct 'question' word.

How   What   When   Where   Who   Why

1. _____ did you put the sweets?
2. _____ is Anna crying?
3. _____ is ringing the bell?
4. _____ is in that jar?
5. _____ did Mansa go to town?
6. _____ do you do?

 C Read the questions. Write the answers.

1. What is your name?

   _____

2. Where do you live?

   _____

3. When do you go to school?

   _____

4. Why do you go to school?

   _____

Reading

A Read the story. Colour the picture.

Fire Wrapped in Paper
(a traditional story from China)

There was once a father who lived with his sons and their wives. The wives were homesick. The father said they could go home if they each brought him back a present. He told the first wife to bring him fire wrapped in paper. He told the second wife to bring him the wind in a piece of paper and the third wife to bring him music in the wind.

On the way home, they met a girl. They told her about their problem. The girl told the first wife to buy a paper lantern. "When you light it, it will be fire wrapped in paper." She told the second wife to buy a paper fan. "When you flap it, it will make the wind in a piece of paper." She told the third wife to buy some wind chimes. "When the wind blows, they will make music in the wind."

Activities

A Write **yes** or **no**.

1. The father lived with his sons and their wives. _____
2. The wives were homesick. _____
3. The father said they could not go home. _____
4. The father wanted paper wrapped in the wind. _____
5. On their way home, the wives met a girl. _____
6. The girl knew what to do. _____

B Write the correct word. Colour the pictures.

fan   wind chimes   lantern   wives

Word Endings: 'ck'

A Ring the correct word.

(sock) / sack / lock	lock / rock / sock	sock / luck / lock
peck / deck / neck	sack / back / suck	deck / duck / luck

B Write the missing letter.

l__ck	b__ck	p__ck
J__ck	s__ck	p__ck
l__ck	s__ck	p__ck

Grammar

 A Unscramble and write these sentences. Do not forget capital letters!

1. is tom going school to.

2. tomorrow going to we town are.

3. will i seven be june in.

4. friend my Emma in is Spain.

5. have i banana a lunch for.

6. go I on Friday holiday on

 B Write **was** or **were** in the space.

1. The book _____ lost.

2. The boys _____ very hungry.

3. The dishes _____ broken.

4. Ann _____ small but Sam and Dan _____ much bigger.

5. They _____ very glad to be home.

6. We _____ at the shop.

Reading

A Read about tigers. Colour the picture.

Tigers

Tigers live in Asia. Most tigers live in forests but so live in swamps.

Tigers are the biggest cats in the world. They are very strong. They have long tails to help them balance. They have orange and black stripes. No two tigers have the same markings. Their markings help them to hide in the forest.

Tigers hunt mainly at night. They eat lots of different animals. Tigers are good swimmers. If the weather gets too hot they go in the water to cool down.

Tiger cubs are born blind. They drink their mother's milk for six to eight weeks. They live with their mother for about two years. She teaches them how to hunt.

Activities

A Write **yes** or **no**.

1. Tigers live in Africa. _____
2. Tigers have stripes. _____
3. Tigers hunt mainly at night. _____
4. Tigers are not good swimmers. _____
5. Baby tigers are called cubs. _____
6. Cubs live with their mother for about two years. _____

B Try this wordsearch.

tiger   animals
forest   hunt
strong   swimmer
stripes   cubs

h	u	m	i	s	h	q	u
u	s	a	s	t	l	u	f
n	w	n	s	r	s	e	o
t	i	i	t	i	g	e	r
g	m	m	r	p	p	k	e
p	m	a	o	e	t	m	s
u	e	l	n	s	n	m	t
e	r	s	g	c	u	b	s

Word Endings: 'ing'

A Write the correct letter for each picture.

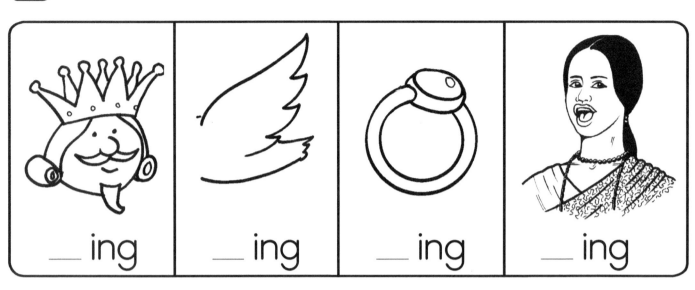

_ing   _ing   _ing   _ing

B Add **ing** to make new words.

play __playing__   talk _____

try _____   tell _____

drink _____   eat _____

sing _____   sleep _____

call _____   fix _____

walk _____   read _____

C Write the missing words. Use the words above.

1. I am _____ to read my book.

2. Abdul is _____ a game.

3. Emma is _____ her lunch.

4. Mum is _____ a song.

5. The baby is _____ in her cot.

6. Dad is _____ to Uncle Ben.

Grammar

 A Write these sentences correctly. Do not forget capital letters!

1. i live in town.

   _____

2. tom and meg are eating.

   _____

3. we have no school on saturday.

   _____

4. i am going shopping today.

   _____

5. ben and sam are going to spain.

   _____

6. aditi will be seven in june.

   _____

 B Write **where** or **were**.

1. Tom knows _____ Emma is.

2. We _____ told to go home.

3. _____ are you going?

4. Ben and Sam _____ at the match.

5. I can't see _____ my hat is.

6. You and I _____ the best at reading.

Reading

A Read the story. Colour the picture.

The Real Princess

Once upon a time, there lived a prince. He wanted to marry a real princess.

One wet, windy night the queen heard a knock on the door. Outside stood a princess who was very, very wet. She said that she was a real princess.

"We will see about that!" thought the queen. The queen made up a bed for the princess to sleep in. On the bed she put three little peas. On top of the peas she put twenty mattresses.

The next morning the queen asked the princess how she had slept. "I slept very badly," cried the princess. "There was something hard under me. Now I am bruised all over."

"This is a real princess," said the queen. "She felt the peas under the twenty mattresses." So the prince and the real princess got married.

Activities

A   Write **yes** or **no**.

1. The prince wanted to marry a queen. _____
2. A very wet princess knocked at the door. _____
3. The queen put three bees on the bed. _____
4. The queen put twenty mattresses on top of the peas. _____
5. The princess slept very well. _____
6. The prince and princess got married. _____

B   Write the missing words. Colour the picture.

Once there was a _____ who wanted to marry a _____ princess. One wet, windy _____, a princess knocked on the _____. She said she was a real _____. The _____ did not think she was a real princess. She made up a _____ for the princess but put three _____ on it. She put twenty _____ on top of the three peas. The next morning the princess told the queen that she had slept very _____. She said that there had been something very _____ under her. Then the queen knew that the _____ was a real princess. The prince had found his real princess and they got _____.

Phonics

A Ring the correct initial sounds.

(br) — dr	pr — cr	gr — dr
fr — dr	pr — gr	pr — cr
tr — fr	dr — br	gr — cr
pr — gr	fr — pr	tr — pr

B Write the correct word under each picture.

stamp swing flag clock star plum drum glass grass

swing	_____	_____
_____	_____	_____
_____	_____	_____

Questions

A Write a question mark.

1. Where is your sister today
2. What are you eating
3. Will we play football on Saturday
4. Who ate all my dinner
5. Why is Tom still in bed
6. Do you like apples and oranges

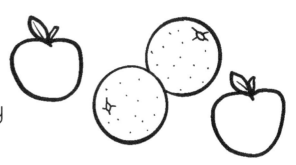

B Write the correct 'question' word.

How   What   When   Where   Who   Why

1. _____ are you going on holiday?
2. _____ did you talk to?
3. _____ is your broken leg?
4. _____ did you take my apple?
5. _____ will the dinner be ready?
6. _____ did you do with the book?

C Write a question mark or a full stop.

1. I know all my tables
2. Do you have any sweets left
3. He does not know his spellings
4. What is your name
5. Where do you live
6. The window is broken

Reading

 Read about chimpanzees. Colour the picture.

Chimpanzees

Chimpanzees are sometimes called 'chimps'. Chimps are friendly, playful animals. They have very strong hands and feet for swinging from branch to branch. Chimps love bananas. An adult chimp can eat about forty bananas at one time!

A baby chimp is carried by its mother until five months old. Then it learns how to walk. It stays close to its mother until it is four years old.

Chimps spend a lot of time combing each other's hair. They use their lips, teeth and fingers. In this way they get rid of dust and insects.

When chimps meet they kiss, rub noses or smile to show that they are friends.

The chimp is a clever animal. It can be taught tricks.

Activities

A Write **yes** or **no**.

1. The chimp is a dangerous animal. _____
2. Chimps eat a lot of bananas. _____
3. A baby chimp learns to walk at five months. _____
4. Chimps use a brush to comb each other's hair. _____
5. The chimp is a clever animal. _____
6. The chimp can be taught to read. _____

B Write the missing words. Colour the picture.

Sometimes chimpanzees are called 'chimps'. Chimps are friendly, _____ animals. They have strong hands and feet for _____ from branch to _____ . A mother chimp carries the baby chimp until it is _____ months old. Then it learns how to _____ but stays by its mother until it is _____ years old. Chimps _____ each other's hair with their lips, teeth and fingers. This helps them to get rid of dust and _____ . When chimps meet each other they kiss, rub noses or _____ . They are _____ animals and can be taught tricks.

Word Endings: 'ss', 'll'

 Write **ss** or **ll**.

we __ __   gu __ __   hi __ __   ki __ __

me __ __   be __ __   hi __ __   fu __ __

 Choose the correct word.

1. Jack and Jill went up the _____ (hill, hall).

2. Emma wants to _____ (mass, pass) her test.

3. The baby gave her doll a _____ (hiss, kiss).

4. I heard a _____ (bell, ball) ringing.

 Write each word in the correct sentence.

tell   ball   fell   well

1. There is no water in the _____ .

2. Ben _____ off the wall.

3. Fu passed the _____ to Lian.

4. "_____ Sam to go to the shop," said Mum.

Capital Letters

 Ring the capital letters.

1. My birthday is next Tuesday.
2. I went with Sam to Paris.
3. My favourite day is New Year's Day.
4. Lions live in Africa.
5. I am going to Japan in June.
6. Frank comes from Australia.

 Write these sentences correctly. Do not forget the capital letters!

1. tom's birthday is in april.

_____

2. when i go to pakistan i will buy you a present.

_____

3. penguins live in antarctica.

_____

4. tonga is in the pacific ocean.

_____

5. last monday i went for a walk.

_____

6. i went to jafar's house on wednesday.

_____

Reading

 Read about sheep. Colour the picture.

Sheep

Sheep are shy animals. They all eat together and rest together. A group of sheep is called a flock.

Some sheep live on hill farms. The farmer on a hill farm uses a sheepdog to collect the flock of sheep. The flock is moved from place to place.

The mother sheep is called a ewe. The father sheep is called a ram. Baby sheep are called lambs. They are born in the spring. When lambs are about three weeks old they start to play together.

As the weather gets warmer the farmer shears the sheep's wool. Coats, scarves and gloves are made from wool. Wool keeps us warm.

A sheep's skin is used to make rugs and slippers.

Activities

A Match the words to make sentences.

Sheep eat together	is called a ewe.
Some sheep live	in the spring.
The mother sheep	the sheep's wool.
The father sheep	is called a ram.
Lambs are born	on hill farms.
The farmer shears	and rest together.

(Sheep eat together → and rest together.)

B Write **yes** or **no**.

1. Sheep are dangerous animals. _____
2. A group of sheep is called a litter. _____
3. A mother sheep is called a ewe. _____
4. A father sheep is called a bull. _____
5. Lambs are born in autumn. _____
6. Sheepdogs look after cows. _____
7. We get wool from sheep. _____
8. A sheep's skin is used to make tea. _____

C Write the correct word. Colour the pictures.

Phonics

 A Write the correct final sounds.

lk　　nt　　nd　　mp　　sk　　st　　sp　　lt.

ha __ __	te __ __	wa __ __
la __ __	ma __ __	fi __ __
ju __ __	pu __ __	be __ __
ba __ __	mi __ __	ne __ __

 B Choose the correct word for each sentence.

pump　　hump　　nest　　lost　　wasp　　sand

1. The _____ stung Ben.
2. The baby bird hid in the _____ .
3. I need a _____ for the flat tyre.
4. The little boy got _____ in the shop.
5. I made a castle in the _____ .
6. The camel has one _____ .

Compound Words

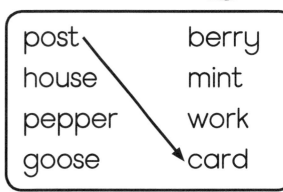

A Match two words. Write the new word.

sea	cake	post	berry
pan	keeper	house	mint
night	gull	pepper	work
goal	mare	goose	card

_____   _____
_____   _____
_____   _____
_____   _____

B Ring the two short words in these words. Write them.

1. (step)(mother) = __step__ + __mother__
2. greenhouse = _____ + _____
3. newspaper = _____ + _____
4. seasick = _____ + _____
5. pineapple = _____ + _____
6. cartwheel = _____ + _____
7. lighthouse = _____ + _____
8. kidnap = _____ + _____

Reading

A Read about the hedgehog. Colour the picture.

The Hedgehog

The hedgehog has sharp, brown spines on his back. His legs are very short.

His home is in a hole in a ditch. It is made of leaves, moss and dry grass.

Baby hedgehogs are born in the summer. For the first four weeks their coats are soft.

The hedgehog hunts at night. If a fox or a person comes close to him he rolls himself into a ball. His spines stick out all over him and no one can touch him.

The hedgehog eats snails, slugs and other garden pests. The hedgehog does not store food for the winter. He sleeps on a bed of dry leaves until spring. This is called hibernation.

Activities

 Write **yes** or **no**.

1. The hedgehog has soft spines on his back. _____
2. The hedgehog has long legs. _____
3. The hedgehog makes his home in a hole in a ditch. _____
4. Baby hedgehogs are born in winter. _____
5. The hedgehog hunts at night. _____
6. The hedgehog eats pizza. _____

 Unscramble the letters to make a word.

1. nispes _____
2. mmsuer _____
3. imanal _____
4. dgaren _____
5. erhibantino _____
6. aisnls _____
7. rispng _____
8. ogehedhg _____

C Finish drawing the hedgehog.

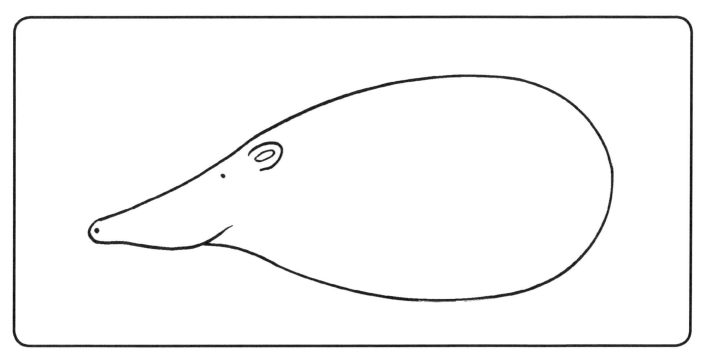

Final Blends

A Ring the correct word for each picture.

nets (nest)	desk pest	skin mask
tent bent	bend wind	belt felt
dump lamp	rest test	tent tank

B Try this wordsearch.

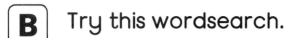

pest	sulk
risk	send
wink	mist
best	dent
bump	help

s	u	l	k	g	d	e	i
p	k	u	l	h	e	l	p
e	f	s	e	n	d	m	c
s	t	r	o	w	i	n	k
t	m	i	s	t	e	j	s
y	n	s	l	d	e	n	t
o	x	k	h	u	v	o	i
b	e	s	t	b	u	m	p

Compound Words

A Match two words. Write the new word.

home	ball
milk	house
foot	work
farm	pot
tea	man

black	brush
hedge	board
arm	chair
lady	bird
hair	hog

_____
_____
_____
_____
_____

_____
_____
_____
_____
_____

B Ring the two short words in these words. Write them.

1. (basket)(ball)   =   basket + ball
2. lighthouse   =   _____ + _____
3. keyhole   =   _____ + _____
4. snowman   =   _____ + _____
5. rainbow   =   _____ + _____
6. starfish   =   _____ + _____
7. raindrop   =   _____ + _____
8. blindfold   =   _____ + _____

Reading

A Read the story. Colour the picture.

The Crow and the Jug

Once there was a very thirsty crow. She looked everywhere for water but could not find any. At last she saw an old jug that had some water in the bottom of it. The crow pushed her beak down into the jug. She pushed and pushed but she could not get near the water.

There were stones near the jug. The crow had an idea. She picked up one stone and dropped it into the jug. The water moved up higher in the jug. The crow picked up another stone and dropped it into the jug. The water in the jug moved up higher still. She picked up another stone and another.

The crow kept dropping stones into the jug. At last the water had moved to the top of the jug. The crow was able to have a drink. She drank and drank until she was no longer thirsty. The crow thought that she was very clever.

Activities

A Match the words to make sentences.

Once there was — a very thirsty crow.
She could not get — down into the jug.
The water moved up — stones into the jug.
The crow kept dropping — higher in the jug.
The crow was able — to have a drink.
The crow pushed her beak — near the water.

B Write the correct sentence under each picture.

The crow saw an old jug with water in it.
The crow pushed her beak down into the jug.
The crow dropped a stone into the jug.
At last the crow was able to have a drink.

Final Blends

A Try this crossword.

Across

1. la___ (lamp)
4. te___ (tent)
7. d_st (dust)
9. ___st (nest)
11. ___lk (milk)
14. li___ (lift)
15. _lf (elf)

Down

1. li___ (list)
2. po___ (pond)
3. be___ (belt)
5. ta___ (tank)
6. wa___ (wasp)
8. si___ (sink)
10. p_nk (pink)
12. h_lf (half)
13. te___ (test)

Grammar

A Write these sentences correctly. Do not forget capital letters and full stops!

1. ben went to see his friend emma

2. jacob will be in lagos on saturday

3. my birthday is in april

4. i am going to dubai in march

5. bob is six and so am i

6. this sunday i am having a party

B Write a **question mark** or a **full stop**.

1. How is your uncle today
2. I will be seven in March
3. Where is the other show
4. Why are you so angry
5. What is wrong with you
6. Meg won the race

Reading

 Read the story.

The Fox and the Goat

Once there was a fox who fell into a well. He tried to get out but he kept falling back down. Soon a rabbit came to drink from the well. The fox asked the rabbit to help him but the rabbit ran away. Soon a sheep came to drink from the well. The fox asked the sheep to help him but the sheep ran away. Soon a goat came to drink from the well. The fox knew the goat would not help him. He knew he would have to try and trick the goat.

"Mr Goat," said the fox, "the water in the well is lovely! Come on down and I'll give you some." The goat was very thirsty and he jumped into the well. The fox jumped onto the goat's horns and climbed out of the well.

"How will I get out of the well?" cried the goat.

The fox was a kind fox. He put the bucket down into the well. The goat climbed in and the fox pulled up the bucket.

"Thank you, Mr Fox," said the goat.

"Next time," said the fox, "look before you leap."

Activities

A Write **yes** or **no**.

1. Once upon a time, a sheep fell into a well. _____
2. The rabbit helped the fox. _____
3. The sheep ran away. _____
4. The fox played a trick on the goat. _____
5. The goat jumped into the well. _____
6. The fox left the goat in the well. _____

B Unscramble these sentences and write them correctly.

1. fox a fell well into A.

   _____

2. The ran sheep away.

   _____

3. rabbit help not would the fox The.

   _____

4. fox put the bucket well the into The.

   _____

C Write the names of the animals.

Word Endings: 'all'

A Write the missing letter for each word.

| t all | w all | b all |
| f all | c all | h all |

B Write **yes** or **no**.

1. The tall man is to make a call. _____
   The ball will fall off the wall. _____

2. The cat is in the hall. _____
   The ball is in the hall. _____

3. The small dog has a ball. _____
   The tall girl is in the hall. _____

4. The small ball is on the wall. _____
   If I fall, I will call. _____

Using Words

A Write **would** or **wood**.

Examples: I put some **wood** on the fire.
I **would** like to go home.

1. I _____ like to go to Egypt on holiday.
2. The table is made of _____ .
3. Pabla _____ not eat his lunch.
4. The _____ has lots of flowers in it.
5. Who _____ like more cake?
6. She _____ not play with me.

B Ring the two short words in these words. Write them.

1. ⓢⓤⓝⓢⓔⓣ = sun + set
2. passport = _____ + _____
3. tracksuit = _____ + _____
4. trapdoor = _____ + _____
5. sunflower = _____ + _____
6. blackbird = _____ + _____
7. supermarket = _____ + _____
8. scarecrow = _____ + _____

Reading

A Write the missing words.

road circus Mum Dad hats town trunk
clowns trousers van lions elephant

The Circus Comes to Town

Meg and Tom were in _____ . The circus parade came up the _____ . The _____ came first. They had baggy _____ and tall red _____ . Everybody laughed at the _____ . Along came a big _____ . The _____ were in the _____ . The _____ has a long _____ . "Please _____ and _____ , may we go to the _____ ?" asked Meg and Tom.

Activities

A Write the correct word.

1. Tom and Meg were in _____. (school, hospital, town)
2. The _____ (band, car, circus) came up the road.
3. The _____ (elephant, lions, clowns) came first.
4. The clowns had _____ (short, baggy, long) trousers.
5. Everybody _____ (cried, laughed, looked) at the clowns.
6. There were _____ (dogs, cats, lions) in the van.
7. An _____ (elephant, lion, cat) has a long trunk.
8. The circus makes me _____. (happy, sad, angry)

B Try this wordsearch.

circus   trousers
town   van
parade   lion
road   elephant
clowns   trunk

e	l	e	p	h	a	n	t
j	l	r	o	a	d	y	r
m	i	k	l	v	a	n	o
t	o	w	n	c	d	a	u
r	n	c	i	r	c	u	s
u	h	n	l	o	s	a	e
n	p	a	r	a	d	e	r
k	g	c	l	o	w	n	s

C Write the correct word under each picture.

_ _ _ _

_ _ _ _ _ _

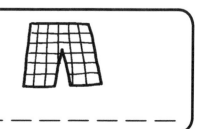
_ _ _ _ _ _ _ _

Word Endings 'Y'

A Write the missing letter for each word.

holl __   tedd __   sunn __   bab __

sand __   mumm __   napp __   bunn __

B Write the missing word. Use the words above.

1. Tom has a new yellow _____ .
2. The _____ is crying.
3. I saw a _____ hopping in the park.
4. There are red berries on the _____ .
5. It is a very _____ day.
6. Our baby has a clean _____ .
7. The beach is nice and _____ .
8. My _____ has a necklace.

Grammar

A Circle the words which should begin with a capital letter. Add full stops.

1. christmas day is in december
2. my dog's name is molly
3. i gave ted a book for christmas
4. i have a goldfish called jaws
5. ben went to london with emma
6. mum said i had to play with tom

B Write a question mark or a full stop.

1. What did the rabbit say to the fox
2. I have an apple for my lunch
3. Why did the chicken cross the road
4. When will the hedgehog wake up

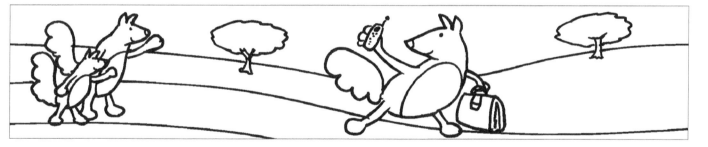

C Write **there** or **their**.

1. They put on _____ coats.
2. The rabbit is over _____ .
3. We are going _____ on Monday.
4. I see a mouse over _____ .
5. I like _____ teacher.
6. _____ cat's had kittens.

Reading

 Read the story.

Taking a Donkey to Market

(a traditional story from Cambodia)

An old man and his son took their donkey to market. It was a long way. They didn't want the donkey to get thin, so they carried him. On the way they met some villagers. "Look at those stupid people carrying a donkey!" they said. "Why doesn't the old man ride it?"

So the son led the donkey and the old man rode it. Later, they met some girls. "Why do you let that old man boss you around?" they asked the son. "You should ride the donkey, not him." So the old man walked and his son rode. Later, they met a farmer. "What a bad son," said the farmer. "You should let your father ride." So the old man got on the donkey behind his son. Later they met a young boy. "That poor donkey," he said. "He's not strong enough to carry both of you."

So the old man and his son got off and walked behind the donkey. When they got to market everyone laughed at them. "How stupid to walk when you've got a donkey!" they said.

"Whatever we do, someone tells us we are doing the wrong thing," said the old man. "Next time I won't listen to what other people say. I shall make my mind up for myself."

Activities

A Unscramble these sentences and write them correctly.

1. took the market They donkey to.

   _____

2. at laughed Everyone them.

   _____

3. they Later farmer a met.

   _____

4. the walked donkey They behind.

   _____

B Write the missing word.

Phonics

A Ring the correct word.

crib / (crab) / trap	dress / pram / drum	stop / star / stag
frog / flag / slug	rock / lock / sock	plug / frog / flag
ring / wing / king	sing / ring / wing	bull / bell / ball
wing / wall / well	milk / mask / wasp	holly / nappy / teddy

Grammar

 A Write these sentences correctly. Do not forget capital letters and full stops!

1. pancho's birthday is in december

_____

2. my friend's name is molly

_____

3. i gave ted a book on friday

_____

4. mum said i had to play with ramesh

_____

5. ben went to mombasa with emma

_____

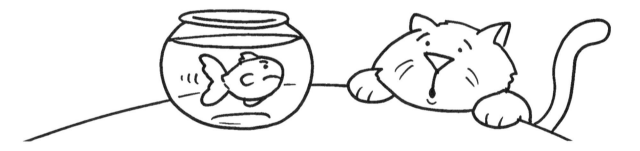

 B Write **their** or **there**.

1. The goldfish bowl is over _____ .

2. The children went to the park on _____ bikes.

3. _____ dog had puppies.

4. I see a cat over _____ .

5. _____ is a frog in _____ garden pond.

Puzzle Page

A Read the clues and complete the words. Then do the crossword.

Across

1. You can carry water in this _ucke_ (6)

6. One chick, two _hick_ (6)

7. You get wool from these __eep (5)

8. A ___ barks (3)

9. Hens lay these e__s (4)

11. Meow! I like milk _a_ (3)

Down

1. You sweep with this __ush (5)

2. The farmer drives this __actor (7)

3. A sh__ sails on the sea (4)

4. We write with this _nk (3)

5. We get eggs from these _ens (4)

10. This is a Billy _oat (4)